A Corner in the World

A CORNER *in the* WORLD

Holocaust Poems for My Father

AYALA ZARFJIAN

2021
GOLDEN DRAGONFLY PRESS

FIRST PRINT EDITION, July 2021
FIRST EBOOK EDITION, July 2021

Copyright © 2021 by Ayala Zarfjian.
All rights reserved.
No part of this publication may be reproduced
or transmitted in any form or by any means, electronic
or otherwise, without prior written permission
by the copyright owner.

ISBN-13: 978-1-7330099-7-3
Library of Congress Control Number: 2021942017

Printed on acid-free paper supplied by a
Forest Stewardship Council-certified provider.
First published in the United States of America
by Golden Dragonfly Press, 2021.

www.goldendragonflypress.com

TO THOSE THAT CAME BEFORE

For my great grandparents Dov and Rene. Murdered.

For Saba Naftali. A hero that saved 15 souls.

For My father that never forgot yet lived his life to the fullest.

For Aunt Shelley for sharing her memories and her story.

For MOM and her ETERNAL LOVE.

For SAFTA DORA for her courage.

For SABA YANCU and SAFTA GINCA for everything.

For my UNCLES and AUNTS for their stories.

TO THOSE THAT CAME AFTER

JOSHUA
DANIEL
IRINA
AIDEN
SOPHIA

TO MY BELOVED CARL
For Gluing the Pieces of Existence

What follow are the current best estimates of civilians and captured soldiers killed by the Nazi regime and its collaborators.

These estimates are calculated from wartime reports generated by those who implemented Nazi population policy, and postwar demographic studies on population loss during World War II.

NUMBER OF DEATHS

Group	Number of Deaths
Jews	6 million
Soviet civilians	around 7 million (including 1.3 Soviet Jewish civilians, who are included in the 6 million figure for Jews)
Soviet prisoners of war	around 3 million (including about 50,000 Jewish soldiers)
Non-Jewish Polish civilians	around 1.8 million (including between 50,000 and 100,000 members of the Polish elites)
Serb civilians (on the territory of Croatia, Bosnia and Herzegovina)	312,000
People with disabilities living in institutions	up to 250,000
Roma (Gypsies)	between 250,000 and 500,000
Jehovah's Witnesses	around 1,900
Repeat criminal offenders and so-called asocials	at least 70,000
German political opponents and resistance activists in Axis-occupied territory	undetermined
Homosexuals	hundreds, possibly thousands (possibly also counted in part under the 70,000 repeat criminal offenders and so-called asocials noted above)

Source: United States Holocaust Memorial Museum

JEWISH LOSS BY LOCATION OF DEATH

Location of Death	Jewish Losses
Auschwitz complex (including Birkenau, Monowitz, and subcamps)	approximately 1 million
Treblinka 2	approximately 925,000
Belzec	434,508
Sobibor	at least 167,000
Chelmno	at least 167,000
Shooting operations at various locations in central and southern German-occupied Poland (the Government General)	at least 200,000
Shooting operations in German-annexed western Poland (District Wartheland)	at least 20,000
Deaths in other facilities that the Germans designated as concentration camps	at least 150,000
Shooting operations and gas wagons at hundreds of locations in the German-occupied Soviet Union	at least 1.3 million
Shooting operations in the Soviet Union (German, Austrian, Czech Jews deported to the Soviet Union)	approximately 55,000
Shooting operations and gas wagons in Serbia	at least 15,088
Shot or tortured to death in Croatia under the Ustaša regime	23,000–25,000
Deaths in ghettos	at least 800,000
Other	at least 500,000

Source: United States Holocaust Memorial Museum

*"First they came for the socialists, and I did not speak out—
    Because I was not a socialist.*

*Then they came for the trade unionists, and I did not speak out—
    Because I was not a trade unionist.*

*Then they came for the Jews, and I did not speak out—
    Because I was not a Jew.*

Then they came for me—and there was no one left to speak for me."

—Martin Niemöller

"Everybody is somebody's Jew."

—Primo Levi

"People get discouraged. They should remember, from me, it takes courage not to be discouraged."

—Ben Ferencz
The last Nuremberg prosecutor alive.

Contents

Grandma's Slippers	1
The Rubble	2
Beloved Uncle	3
Sally	4
Not Anonymous	5
Slaughterhouse	6
The Lillies	7
Fractured	8
The Sound of Thunder	9
Silence	10
Moral Compass	12
Great Grandparents	13
Aunt Shelley	14
Photographs	15
The Convoy	16
The Frog	17
My Sister	18
The Death Wagon	19
Saplings	20
Brave	21
Hair	22
Roots	23
Mamaliga	24
The Truth at Twelve	25
The Jew	26

Afterward	27
Jidan	28
Uncle	29
Layers and Layers	31
The Snowflake	32
Small Miracle	33
The Dream	34
Little Bird	35
Bitter	36
School	37
Cloudscapes	38
Borders	39
Warriors	40
In the Light of the Moon	42
The Hero	43
Restore	44
Liberation	45
Did He See Me?	46
Liberation	47
The Questions	49
Grandfather's Silence	50
A Mountain	51
The Beets	52
Veins	53
It Can Happen Again	54
Human	55
Auschwitz	56
Slaughtered	57
The Ball	58
Sara	59

Two Hands	61
Ancestry	62
The Righteousness Among Nations	63
Transnistria	64
Mourn	65
Acknowledgments	67

Grandma's Slippers

Powder blue or green.
Open-toed or closed.
Soft or hardened.
I do not know.
I do not know of grandma's
House slippers,
Their texture or their color.
I imagine they were worn out.
Beauty faded,
coziness lost,
disintegrated,
and colorless
by the time grandma was liberated from the camp.
In the end,
her shoes were gone.
Only the house slippers remained.
In the middle of the night,
I awaken,
haunted by the vision of
Grandma cold.
Grandma shoeless.
Grandma an adult orphan of the war.

The Rubble

For Safta Ginca

The rubble held their past.
Pieces of a family,
of faith,
of love.
They stood on the sidewalk,
their hearts racing in their throats.
They trembled from the sight,
the sound, the roar.
Shaking from ingesting the smell of
charred wood, smoldering corpses,
blood, and destruction.
An ordinary Wednesday,
until it no longer was.
A pivotal moment in their life.
The house was bombed.
The walls crumbled to the ground.
The glass shattered and dispersed.
I wonder, was there tea brewing in the teapot?
Were there sugar cookies baking in the oven?
Was grandfather reading a book by Chekhov?
The sirens went off
for a second time that day.
A scheduled and passive exercise.
Did grandmother hear the sky shaking?
Did she listen to the roar of the planes,
heavy with intention?
Was it her intuition that
propelled her to run?
Run with her husband,
daughter, and son.
Run toward life.

Beloved Uncle

For Uncle Jan Eckhaus

If I could envision
your form.
The way your arms stretched endlessly.
The way you hoisted me in the air
spontaneously.
The way your eyes lit up
like constellations in the sky
when I ran to greet you at the door.
Your smile, wide and joyous,
rising from within your core.
I rouse up memories,
but I can't recall the sound of your voice.
It escapes me,
lost in an endless void.
We don't have a picture of you.
Not one.
As evidence that you,
a handsome and wise man, ever existed.
Beloved Uncle,
one morning you departed,
never to return to our awaiting arms.
Your blood
on their hands.
Your blood spilled.
The soil absorbing
the sweetness and kindness of you.
The earth weeping along with us.

Sally

For Aunt Sally Eckhaus

I no longer remember the sound of her laughter.
I no longer remember the scent of her perfume.
Did she bake challah for the sabbath?
Did her hands form a perfect braid?
The wind whispered her name.
Her hair flowed when she walked.
Darkness, illuminated by her smile.
She embraced her husband for the last time.
The memories of their newlywed days sustained her.
Their faces beamed when they found each other in a crowd.
Their hearts beat as one.
Their unconscious flowing tenderness was seamless.
A dance of life, filled with beauty and kindness.
Sally mourned my beloved uncle's death.
Devastated and alone she returned
to reclaim their home.
The villagers that pillaged their possessions
took her life.
Her body was dismembered.
I imagine all the places where
the parts were thrown.
Patches of beautiful lilies grew there.

Not Anonymous

I see your drawing on the wall
of block 27.
An empty baby carriage
for your doll.
The doll with light brown hair
and hazel eyes.
Wearing a mustard yellow dress
with a navy blue collar.
What did you name her?
Rebecca or Gitty,
Shayna or Deborah.
I will never know.
I envision you before your life was taken.
In a lush garden, singing while you hopscotched
as you embraced your doll.
A vivacious child
with a beautiful name and
soft, delicate hands.
Your hair swayed when you jumped and ran,
your spirit full of light.
You are not anonymous.
Your life is remembered.
Your drawing displayed as testimony.
Your world ours.
Your pencil lines etched in our consciousness.

Slaughterhouse

In the slaughterhouse
they hung them on butcher's hooks.
Heavy stainless-steel hooks that
pierced their skin as they were tortured.
In the place where carcasses once hung,
now men hung,
ordinary men.
Deep and jagged wounds formed.
Bleeding and tormented,
they felt the pain invading
their senses.
Afterward,
their stomachs were cut open,
their entrails roped around their
bleeding necks.
The sign screamed Kosher meat.

The Lillies

Lilies are blooming
in the place that you are buried.
Even though I will never know,
I am certain of it.
Dismembered,
your pieces strewn
into the soil,
into an unmarked grave
and place.
No one comes to recite the Kaddish for you.
I often think of your hands,
soft and delicate,
how you pressed them into my palm.
Your laughter robust
with the joy of being alive.
The lilies grow and weep,
for your loss
and ours.

Fractured

The rain saturated
our clothes.
The wetness seeped into our bones.
Our bodies were defenseless.
The convoy stopped at the
border of Bessarabia.
We were ordered to relinquish
gold, silver, anything of value.
A collective trepidation was felt
as people sighed.
Mother held a valise
with cherished family photographs of
her children,
of her murdered parents.
The German officer barked at her.
His voice harsh, jagged.
Mother opened her mouth to explain.
He raised his heavy belt to strike her.
Father came between them.
The blow smashed his finger.
Father's eyes filled with anguish.
His affliction registered on his face.
Father was a strong man.
A mighty man.
My heart tightened.
The valise was taken away.
The astonishment of
the senseless violence
never dissolved.
Father's finger remained fractured
all his life.

The Sound of Thunder

It was the sound of thunder
cutting through the air,
cutting through our existence.
The fourteen-year-old boy
was caught selling apples
that he bartered for.
The German officer's face was dark,
ruthless,
evil.
He took the boy and, sadistically,
he tied him to the horse.
The horse galloped with urgency and speed,
pulling the boy to his death.
Fourteen years old,
his spirited being was
silenced.
A gruesome end to a young life.
Our hands tied,
the sound of torture reverberating through
our days.
The pain seared long after we digested the hopelessness
that we encountered,
and lived through.

Silence

Twenty years after the war,
the boy was a man.
A man with branches of his own.
A family.
The shadows of his younger life
lurked in his subconscious.
Seldom he let the slivers out.
In a sunlit apartment in Tel-Aviv,
the man wrote a story for his daughter.
She inherited his soft curly hair,
his soul of a poet,
and his spirit.
The story he wrote
was about a horse with a broken leg.
When she grew up,
she wondered if the story reflected his brokenness
or her own.
His love of horses
caught him a beating that he would not forget.
Grandfather's hand came down
heavy with fury.
His brows crossed.
Sweat beads on his forehead.
No tolerance afforded.
No empathy offered.
Only fear.
A fear that is in the core of one's marrow.
The pain seared his skin.
The sting remained burning.

Grandfather, terrified by what could have been.
The boy risked his life to touch the horse's mane,
taken by his beauty
and immeasurable strength.
The horse was innocent.
It was his owner that was a sadistic Nazi.
When he rode the horse into the camp,
all the children disappeared.
They knew that he tied the boy to his horse
and dragged him to his death.
They knew the man was soulless
and evil resided behind his vacant eyes.

Moral Compass

The woman knocked on the door.
She asked to come in.
Grandmother let her.
She walked to the table,
the table that the cousins slept on.
The table that the cousins pissed from
onto the concrete floor
when they had typhus.
Stripped of their humanity,
stripped of their dignity.
The woman opened the satchel
that she held in her hand.
The diamonds shimmered,
the gold glistened,
the jewels were abundant.
Possessions robbed from the Jews.
She was the mother of the officer
with the horse.
The officer that tormented the lager.
The murderer.
She begged,
she pleaded for grandfather to accept the riches
of the satchel as payment to not testify against her son.
Grandfather roared and demanded that she leave the house.
The abandoned house where fifteen lives were saved.
The abandoned house without running water or a toilet.
The abandoned house boarded up.
The abandoned house they slept in, on boards on the floor.
On a table.
Three people in a twin bed.
The place that was bare and stripped.
The place that they lived and barely survived, frail and hungry.
Grandfather testified.
His moral compass remained righteous.

Great Grandparents

For Dov and Rene

The windows were covered
with green curtains.
The large white cups and saucers
brimmed with warm milk.
A large dish of heaping cookies,
was on the table.
Grandma's kind offering.
Small details
that sustained us during an unforgiving winter.
A winter laced with sadness and loss.
Faint memories floated through our days.
Shattering news arrived.
Our grandparents murdered.
Their home burnt to the ground.
Grief-stricken we remembered,
their gentle ways.
Their kindness.
Their love.

Aunt Shelley

For Rachel Eckhaus

Her voice tremors.
"The fear never leaves me,"
she says, sobbing.
She is eighty years old.
Her tears show the enormity
of her isolation and anguish.
Her grief palpable.
I visualize her as a little girl,
frightened and hungry.
Stripped of all the familiar things.
Home, identity, and basic dignity.
Her memories tangled in
agony and despair.
Her mother, a tree
with anchoring roots.
Her father, the moon.
Constant, present,
lighting her way through the darkness.
Her brother, her rock.
Their life reduced to nothing.
Their world wounded,
disintegrated.

Photographs

The lens captures the transparent
but not the unseen.
The plight endured,
the journey of our life.
There are
photographs we took
after the war.
But there are no images to summon the memory
of a life lived before.
The life once built and nurtured.
Gone and erased as if it never existed.
There are no photographs of your infancy.
Safe and cradled with love.
There are none of you as a toddler,
with black curly hair and eyes large as grapes.
There are no photographs of you as a young boy,
lighting the universe with your smile.
All taken and eradicated.
The way they meant to eradicate our lives.

The Convoy

The convoy shrinks.
Mothers, fathers, children
shot or left to die as they wilt away.
Fatigue and hunger overtake them.
Abandoned on the road like discarded garbage.
We walk through hell, side by side.
We don't know our destination.
We are like sheep led to slaughter.
We follow the path we are ordered to
or we die.
My little sister abruptly stops.
She is at a standstill, weeping.
Her little feet can't go on.
Father does not dare lift his eyes to the soldiers.
He does not utter a word.
Father hoists her up on his wide shoulders.
Her tresses fall down.
She sits on the blanket that covers his bag.
The bag holds the few possessions that are still ours.
He gathers strength from within.
He finds the will for both of them.

The Frog

The frog
Watches me as I drink
from the rain puddles.
I am thirsty.
I am hungry.
The frog watches me,
his bulging eyes darting
as I scoop more rainwater in the palm of my hand.
The frog looks puzzled.
His neckless body
and hind legs at ease as he croons.
My eyes fill with gratitude and sorrow,
weaving into one emotion within me.
It's raining.
Our convoy stops for the night.
Those that can't keep pace
are shot.
Some are left to die on the side of the road.
My parents are standing under the
shaggy heads of trees.
They are wet and spiritless.
I see fear and anguish in their eyes.
They pretend not to weep.
My sister is sitting nearby.
We will share a wet blanket.
The blanket that father wraps
around his shoulder bag.
One of the few possessions we still have.

My Sister

My sister used to hop joyfully all the way home
from kindergarten.
She repeatedly sang a song
about her doll sitting in a carriage.
A carriage with four wheels.
Her eyes bright,
her cheeks full,
her silky hair flying in the wind.
Our life before it was taken.
Our childhood before it was robbed.
My sister and I forgot how to cry.
Our tears dried up.
She is younger than I.
Her sadness is palpable.
We feel it in our bones.
In our marrow.
Invisible tears
pour out of us.
Our faces dry.
Our eyes averted.
Our screams silent.

The Death Wagon

Day after day,
I sat by the boarded window.
An open sliver,
a porthole to the outside.
Day after day,
I heard the horse's neigh,
before I saw the death wagon
passing by.
The wagon stopped on its way
to hoist bodies from the soiled snow.
Bodies thrown and piled up callously,
with lack of dignity or burden.
I pondered if the horse witnessed the horrors.
Did the horse weep
the way I wept,
remembering what it felt like
to be myself?
Remembering brushing my hair before bedtime.
Holding my doll to my chest.
Her hair black as mine.
Both of us nestled in bed.
Home.
The walls embracing our presence.
Mom, dad, and my brother's joyful voices
echoing from the adjoining room.
All an evaporated memory.

Saplings

1.5 million saplings
cut down.
Their roots pulled from
the ground before
they fully lived.
1.5 million saplings that will not grow into trees
to fill the universe with air.
Their leaves will not nourish.
Their leaves will not dance to the brush of the wind,
nor giggle at the touch of the sun.
1.5 million vulnerable saplings,
eradicated by a fatal storm.

1.5 Million children were murdered during the Holocaust.

Brave

Grandfather towered over the stove.
The honey-colored rays of sunshine
entered through the window.
The kitchen was the heart of the small restaurant.
Grandfather fiercely pounded the chicken cutlets
into large pieces before frying them.
His love expressed in the food that he cooked
to nourish others.
Grandfather had a mighty stature and a silent strength.
His roar loud but his silence louder.
Varicose veins mapped his legs and
his large hands.
Grandfather's wounds were fathomless.
On the margins of life he
lived and survived.
On his broken wings he carried the frail home.
He never spoke of his bravery.
He never spoke of the murders of his beloved brother
and kin.
He never spoke of the senseless violence and humiliation.
He never spoke of nearly dying while he was beaten.
His skin raw with black and blue bruises, swollen for days.
His torment was muted.
Remarkable resilience and gratitude emanated from him.

Hair

Two tons of hair.
Wavy,
curly,
straight,
braided.
Two tons of hair displayed at the Auschwitz Museum.
The hair shorn from corpses of women and children
after they were gassed to death.
Traces of cyanide gas used
to exterminate them.
Hair, a fragment of one's identity,
their essence.
A twisted and treacherous story on display.
A story we cannot articulate.
Our words empty at the sheer
enormity of dehumanization.
The hair used to make textiles,
socks, thermal shirts,
ropes, chords,
mechanical parts.
Is that conceivable in anyone's mind?
Two tons on display.
The outrage pours out of us.
We mumble in disbelief.
We look away, not able to digest what we have seen.
Our stomachs in knots.
Our hearts numb.
Shattered.
Two tons.

Roots

Our roots are embedded here,
said my great-grandmother.
She carried seeds of hope in her heart.
A believer in humanity,
soft-spoken and graceful.
Her home was filled with warmth.
The white large cups brimming with warm milk.
Sugar cookies on the table.
Colorful flowers in her front yard.
Paintings on her wall.
Luxurious and soft blankets adorned her bed.
Her strength was palpable.
Her ways were gentle.
Our roots are embedded here, she said.
We ran from persecution and antisemitism.
We left our home behind.
We started over.
We raised our children here.
We have lived here most of our lives, said my great grandmother.
She did not want to leave.
She did not know where they could go.
She carried hope.
And then they came,
they forced their way in.
They shot her and my great grandfather
in cold blood,
and burned their house down.

Mamaliga

Mother stands and stirs
a large pot of boiling water,
grateful for a sprinkle of cornmeal.
It mimics,
Romania's traditional food.
A richness of texture and color
absent here.
Our imagination drifts to a tasteful mamaliga,
on a porcelain plate,
garnished with butter and sour cream.
Flavorful and savory.
This meal diluted,
the way our life is diminished.

The Truth at Twelve

At twelve years old,
I stood at the edge of the world,
Waving into emptiness.
I had never attended a symphony.
I had never seen a whale.
I had not floated in the Black Sea.
I had not kissed a girl.
Life was full of cracks and crevices.
Life was stripped away of all the ordinary.
Life was stripped away of its humanity.
The winds of change
Shifted our lives from all we had known
To the only truth that mattered.
Survival was intimate.
Survival was imminent.
Survival was the only truth we understood.

The Jew

The shock registered on the soldiers' faces.
Shoulder to shoulder
they had served in the army.
Side by side they stood together.
That afternoon, while the cold
seeped into their bones, they recognized
their friend.
The Jew.
To their dismay, he was captive in the lager.
An invisible border was erected between them.
On occasion, they smuggled potatoes and apples
to keep us alive.
Father held the world on his broad shoulders.
15 mouths to feed.
15 souls to keep alive.
In the shadows of his face
there were traces of memory and burden etched.
Did he recite the kaddish for the father he lost
during World War I?
His childhood was stained by loss and absence.
He navigated the uncertainty with his premonition.
His intuition was his savior
and ours.

Afterward

Years after the war,
years after they crawled from death to life,
they found a place to call their own.
The land of milk and honey.
The land abundant with olives and figs,
grapes and pomegranate.
Grandpa and grandma would come to visit
on Saturday afternoons.
The stories leaked
over coffee and cake.
The smell of jasmine floating through the
sunlit windows.
The quiet of the Sabbath was intoxicating.
The stories were not fully formed.
It was a sentence that spoke volumes,
it was a mention that only they understood.
It was a faint remembrance,
stuffed into the subconscious.
The pain resurfaced
with a vengeance.
They submerged it back into
the shadows of the past.
I listened, waiting for the trail of crumbs
that I wished to carry with me.
The whole story.
Never told.
Humiliation.
Deprivation.
Deportation.
Loss.
The harder I listened,
the less was said.
Details taken,
swept away,
for another day.

Jidan

For Uncle Reuven Schvartz

On the train tracks, your blood stains
breathed life into the metal.
Revived it to bear witness
to your affliction.
To the cruelty of your death.
The iron guard fascists
boarded the train.
Their boots heavy.
Their callousness visible.
They threatened and demanded
to discover who was a Jidan.
The slur echoed off the walls.
Their tone dripped with malice.
Their tongue was sharp with venom.
Dread hung in the air,
the way evil coursed through their blood.
Was your skin too fair?
Did-your stature betray you as you sat among
the army friends that attempted to shelter you?
Was your uniform pressed to perfection?
A young engineer with infinite dreams.
A soldier coming home.
Your family was told of the way they ruthlessly flung you
off the train.
The ground shivered.
The wind wept.
A bright light extinguished.

Jidan is a Romanian slur for Jew.

Uncle

Are your ashes here Uncle?
In this building erected in remembrance
the year that I was born.
I, another child that would have not existed
if my kin had not survived.
Are your ashes here Uncle?
In this sanctuary built
for the mourners that have
no place to mourn their immense loss.
Ashes brought here
from the extermination camps.
A place of collective memory.
The eternal flame illuminates the hall
the way your light shined in the universe.
A place for humanity to remember their kin.
They tried to eradicate every memory that
you existed,
unaware that you will never be erased.
Your spirit lives.
Your name will be spoken from one generation
to the next.
We will never forget.

"In 1961, Yad Vashem inaugurated the Hall of Remembrance, the first Holocaust commemoration site established at Yad Vashem on the Mount of Remembrance.

"The Hall is an imposing structure, with walls made of basalt boulders brought from the area surrounding the Sea of Galilee, and an angular roof that gives it a tent-like shape. Engraved on the mosaic floor are the names of 22 of the most infamous Nazi murder sites, symbolic of the hundreds of extermination and concentration camps, transit camps and killing sites that existed throughout Europe.

"The Eternal Flame, burning from a base fashioned like a broken bronze goblet, continuously illuminates the Hall, its smoke exiting the building through an opening at the highest point of the ceiling. Before it stands a stone crypt containing the ashes of Holocaust victims, brought to Israel from the extermination camps."[1]

---

1. United States Holocaust Memorial Museum. "The Hall of Remembrance." Holocaust Encyclopedia. https://www.yadvashem.org/remembrance/commemorative-sites/hall-of-remembrance.html. Accessed on June 11, 2021.

Layers and Layers

In the room hangs a cloud.
Our wounds have scars,
but the lacerations are infected.
Mother stares off into the distance.
The war, a malignant tumor
that remains in her body.
At school I find solace in music.
I beam when I am chosen to be a soloist.
Mother refuses to buy a piano for me.
We no longer buy such things, she says.
The seeds of doubt and fear
are palpable to me.
There are layers and layers between us,
of before and after.
Spaces and pauses and unsaid words.
I imagine mother envisioning her
parents' last moments.
Her mother's hand trembling.
Her wedding ring wrapped around her finger,
the symbol of their love and devotion.
Was it pried off her hand before or after?
Were they murdered at once,
or did they have to watch their beloved die?
The cloud hangs.
Layers and layers between us,
of before and after.

The Snowflake

The snowflake floated
in the air.
Magically it landed in my open palm.
I watched it die.
The beauty of its existence
not lost on me.
Unique and fragile.
For a moment, shedding a soft light.
I knelt down in the snow,
grief saturating my soul.
What is to come of me?
Will I survive to see Spring?
Is my life as fragile as this beautiful departed snowflake?

Small Miracle

On the walk to reclaim our lives,
we stumble on a vineyard.
Grapes, fragrant and sweet,
hanging off the vines.
Smooth-skinned and ripe,
we devour them unwashed.
It is surreal.
We cannot believe our good fortune.
The sweetness stays in our mouths.
Foreign to our lips, it lingers.
For three years, we could not taste
such a delight.
The moment feels sacred.
A small miracle.

The Dream

I lick my lips in my sleep.
In front of me is a blue and white plate.
On it, a generous helping of
chicken, eggplant, and potato.
The smell is intoxicating as it wafts
through our home.
Father is in the kitchen cooking.
I hear the sound of meat searing.
I cannot contain myself,
knowing how delectable the food is.
Knowing it will melt in my mouth and nurture
my body and my soul.
I cannot wait another minute.
I lift the fork to my lips.
Abruptly, I awaken.
I am hungry.
I am in the darkest days of my life.
Home, a distant memory.
The dream hovers,
evoking a bottomless longing.
The bleakness invades and I close
my eyes.
Struggling to fall back asleep.

Little Bird

Little bird,
have you soared high past
the grey forest?
Have you flown to my home?
Have you pressed your beak to the window?
Were the drapes drawn
for you to witness who was dwelling
in my home?
Our soft beds and plush pillows.
Our blankets, luxurious and colorful.
Books, notebooks, and pencils.
Our pantry stocked with grandmother's jam
contained in clear glass jars.
Ruby red cherries
and orange peaches.
Sugar, oil, flour, and tea.
Bars of delectable chocolate.
Such treasures!
Our home.
Our refuge.
A remote dream we cannot indulge in.

Bitter

The day was punctuated with bitterness and sorrow.
Our souls frayed at the seams.
The Germans were losing the war.
The silence in the world community persisted.
The Red Cross was placing children in orphanages
for their safety.
Transport and warm blankets were provided.
Parents signed papers to
send their children away.
One parent was allowed to accompany them.
The day was grievous.
Separating from Mother was bitter.
Her blue eyes, an ocean of sadness.
Her lips trembled. Anguish rising.
Her pulse throbbing.
Father took us on the train.
I cried.
I trembled.
Father wept.
Brother was silent and pensive.
I begged Father to return us back to Mother.
I implored him to take us back to the hell
that we knew and endured.
I urged him to let us live or die with them.
Father, ambivalent and devastated,
succumbed and took us back.

School

We arrive at Dorohoi,
 free but fearful.
The sting remains as
 the venom infiltrates our existence.
The Jewish community had thrived here
 until it was charred to the ground.
 Violence,
 Anti-Semitism.
 Looting.
 Murder.
Peasants stripped the clothes off the lifeless bodies
 lying in the streets.
Jews were deported.
Many died hungry, thirsty,
 unable to breathe in the sealed cars of their transport.
The abandoned school
 was a desolate place.
There were books and notebooks left behind.
 For a fleeting moment the sadness
 that saturates our beings is lifted.
We rejoice to touch the books.
 Feel them
 and open them.
The covers faded, shaking.
We savor the words printed on the dusty pages.
 Their spines trembling to our touch.
 Our stomachs flutter.
 In the deafening silence we reflect.
 Our thoughts drift to the children that were
 in this school.
 Their lives silenced and erased.
The walls are colorless.
The walls are muted, holding in the stories of those gone.

Cloudscapes

The clouds
hang heavy in the sky.
They depict cloudscapes
of shapes and creatures.
The clouds drift off.
They appear and they vanish.
We watch the formations.
We are shackled to these days.
We are captives to the smells and sounds
of despair.
We are swimming in melancholy and tribulation.
Grace is found here
like a glass of salt in a large lake it evaporates.
Small kindness in a vast ocean of bitterness.
The forces outside are powerful.
If I surrender to fear it will destroy me.
Everything shrinks in me.
Hope will carry me through another dawn.

Borders

The borders were blurred
like a house without walls.
A house without windows to look out of,
without doors to enter.
The borders spilled
into peppered territories.
Claimed, bartered, invaded.
Blood stained the soil,
the rivers, the forests.
Violence gutted our existence.
The inheritances reside in our bodies
to this day.
They remain from one generation to the next.
Anguish and sorrow entwined.
Piercing thorns in our hearts.

Warriors

There was no confession uttered.
There was no regret.
Strength was birthed from the struggle.
Ester.
Ella.
Regina.
Roza.
Rebels.
Death was imminent.
Weeks near the end.
Weeks near liberation
 they were hanged.
Executed for treason.
Four fierce women.
Under guard and hiding from prying eyes,
they created a smuggling chain.
Enabled the carrying of small
amounts of gunpowder hidden
on their bodies.
They were a part of the resistance.
Hand grenades were made using empty
sardine cases.
The blow they created was enough to halt
the crematorium.
As it burst into flames,
the smoke rose and hovered over the camp.
The skies darkened.
It was inoperable.
I recite their names.

Ester.
Ella.
Regina.
Roza.
Courageous
and powerful.
Their warrior spirits are undeniable.
They chose to rise.
They chose to fight.
In the black hole of Auschwitz.

Inspired by the revolt at Auschwitz October 1944.
Inspired by these four women:

Ester Wajcblum,
Ella Gärtner,
Regina Safirsztain,
Róza Robota

In the Light of the Moon

I stood in the light of the crescent moon,
I held hope in the palm of my hand.
Hope escaped and floated into the
walls of my heart.
In the chambers of my heart hope flourished.
There were days it grew dark with despair.
I asked hope to carry me through the days
that I was feeble.
I asked hope to carry me through my brokenness.
I had not lived yet.
I did not want to die.
I muted the rumble of hunger that rose from my belly.
I muted the noise of doubt.
I nurtured hope to life.

The Hero

A sigh bounced off the empty walls.
The moment punctuated.
The sound vibrating outwards.
One spoon of soup.
Clear broth.
A moan.
A smack of the lips.
Fifteen mouths to feed.
The spoon glided in.
The spoon glided out.
A sound of gratitude.
One by one he fed them.
One spoon at a time.
The jar emptying.
Gratitude palpable.
He never spoke of the sacrifices.
There was no mention of bravery.
He saved them.
Fifteen souls,
that was enough.

Restore

How do we restore our soul.
How do we wash away our thoughts,
mired and repugnant.
How do we heal our wounds,
deep and penetrating.
How do we rise
to meet life
at a new crossroad,
with the charcoal sky
a constant in our subconscious.
The longing to live propels us,
it leads the way.
Silent poetry nurtures our thoughts.
The soul is the flame
that carries our stories,
our grief,
our desire,
our will to survive.

Liberation

Does life begin at liberation?
A rebirth.
Remembering who you are,
a spiritual being.
How do we wash the
stench of death from our minds.
How do we daydream,
when only nightmares arise.
How do we silence the sounds.
harsh and unforgiving.
How do we quiet the fury.
Does life begin again?

Did He See Me?

Did God see me
hiding behind the bushes.
Invisible.
Did he hear my heart pounding like a drum.
My eyes as open windows
absorbing it all.
Dead bodies stacked
in a mass grave.
My rabbi,
my mentor,
he taught me my bar mitzvah prayers
in this hell hole.
Like a wounded bird,
he was a soft-spoken and gentle man.
He carried faith in his pockets
and in his being.
He hung,
tortured and lifeless.
His wings broken.
His tongue severed.
His eyes gorged.
He was silenced,
never to see the beauty of the scriptures
or bestow kindness on others.
He was eliminated from this world.

Liberation

Near the end,
time hung heavy.
Decay ravaged the hours.
The German and Romanian soldiers
heard the news of the advance
of the Red Army.
They hastily encompassed
the camp with gasoline barrels.
They wanted to scorch all remaining life to the ground.
They wanted no trace of their crimes.
On that day, mayhem ensued.
Shots were fired.
Slightly, we opened a crack in the door,
alarmed by the roar from outside.
"Close the door you dirty Jew!"
barked an enraged voice.
We huddled in silence.
We waited.
We feared.
There was no indication of time until
the fire subsided
and quiet fell, like a soft blanket over the camp.
Grace conquered that day.
We were liberated.
The high-ranking officer was told that
the young boy with the piercing eyes knew
where the mass grave was.
The Soviet officer showed the boy his credentials
and proudly he uttered,
"I am Jewish just like you!"

The boy peered at the man,
his uniform,
and his kind face.
The boy began to absorb that they were free.
He was free.
He would remember that moment all his days.
He led the officer to the mass grave.
The boy had witnessed death and horror.
Bodies stacked with callous indifference.
The officer's voice rose into a deafening roar
as he ordered the captured murderers
to dig through the muck and soil.
They recovered the lifeless bodies
with their bare hands.

The Questions

Afterwards the questions that I pondered were:
Was there dignity in our days of survival?
Did light surface in the infinite darkness?
Was there a quiet desperation leading to insanity?
The days brimmed with melancholy and uncertainty.
Was there dignity rooted in the hunger
that burned within?
In our collective effort to stand shoulder to shoulder.
Our humanity,
our individuality,
blurred.
Threads in pools of desperation.
a kind word,
a clear sky,
a moment of solitude.
The air nourished me.
Hope sustained me.
I could not shrink.
I could not allow myself to disappear.
I wanted to,
but I could not.

Grandfather's Silence

Grandfather is silent,
until he roars.
His eyes shine,
until they darken.
He does not kiss us.
Instead, he smells our heads,
as if he inhales our essence.
He carries his wound with great fortitude,
his courage unclaimed.
He never speaks of the stories of survival.
One story of him and two others
bartering clothes for potatoes in a neighboring
village by the lager.
His two companions killed and grandfather left alive,
promising the soldiers a gold watch.
The soldiers beat him and threw him into a ravine.
Grandmother and the others heard of the shooting.
They waited for hours sick with worry.
At night grandfather was helped to the house.
He collapsed.
His body was raw.
They peeled off their own clothes to cover him
with compresses.
His body, a canvas of black, blue, and purple.
Grandfather with his massive hands
and his open heart.
He survived the war,
but the war lived in him.

A Mountain

The mass grave
was a mountain with a mouth to swallow and amass
bodies.
The mass grave
was without eyes to discriminate
and to weep.

The Beets

The field was plentiful,
with colorful beets
peeking from the moist soil.
Their roots clawed in deeply,
in the partial shade they thrived.
We ran to them joyfully.
Shyly they peeked their heads from the
ground to greet us.
We wiped away the caked-on soil
with our bare hands.
Ravenous we devoured them,
delighted at our fortune.

Veins

The war endures in you.
It lingers in your capillaries,
in your arteries,
in your veins.
The war is a river that bridges the past to the present.
It exists within you like waves that come to the shore
and depart with the outgoing tide.
Only to return time and time again.
The war manifests itself
in the pounding of your heart,
the chambers shaking with what cannot be forgotten.
In dreams that consume you,
in the dark.
It is imprinted indelibly.

It Can Happen Again

"We must be listened to: above and beyond our personal experience, we have collectively witnessed a fundamental unexpected event, fundamental precisely because unexpected, not foreseen by anyone. It happened, therefore it can happen again: this is the core of what we have to say. It can happen, and it can happen everywhere."

— Primo Levi

Tender heart
the sky weeps.
Embers blazing
with fervor.
The metamorphosis has surfaced.
Times have shifted again.
Humanity at a crossroad.
Humanity stood on the sidelines
and bored witness.
Humanity has forgotten
the lessons of the past.
It can happen again.
If we let it.
It can.

Human

Vanilla and chocolate
ice cream.
Soft and creamy.
Will I ever taste your sweetness again?
Divine and splendid.
Melting in my mouth
with distinct pleasure.
My stomach is empty,
my heart is ravaged,
yet I still think of you.
Dreaming of you,
is one of the things that still makes me human.

Auschwitz

The old man touches the ink,
faded and unclear.
He reflects on the day
he was branded.
One by one they stood
in a row.
In alphabetical order.
The numbers tattooed and
ingrained on their skin.
The ink penetrated their soul
in a cold and dark way.
Their identities diminished
and taken away.
The numbers displayed
the details of their journey.
The numbers, unassuming,
swept down on them
like a vulture to its prey
and swallowed them whole.

II

Seventy years of history and pain unravel.
The descendants of Auschwitz survivors
tattoo identification numbers on their arms.
A replica of their grandparents' numbers.
A symbol of survival.
The shame washed away
and worn with pride.
An homage of love and honor.

Slaughtered

The sound of sorrow reverberates from the ground.
It echoes from these walls.
We gaze at the room,
 unable to enter,
 unable to take it all in.
We are paralyzed by the enormity of loss.
 Our stomachs churn.
We feel faint.
 Our skin tingles.
 4.6 million names written,
 recorded,
 memorialized.
 How does one conceive and humanize each life?
 Each life with pockets of dreams, hopes, despair.
One life, a whole world.
A world from birth to unconscionable death.
 Pulled like weeds in an endless field.
A sea of names
 and still more uncounted.
 Families and communities erased.
Wiped out.
 Slaughtered without a trace.
Their names and their testimonies silenced.
 Evaporated.
 Eradicated.

The Ball

The ball was made of rags,
washed and discolored.
The boy led the others
in a game of football.
His face beamed.
Their legs carried them away,
like small ants scurrying.
Away from the dreadfulness that gnawed
on their hours and days.
While they played, they had wings.
The bottomless pit in their stomach did not growl.
The smell of the stench did not saturate their senses.
In that moment
their life was not diminished.
It was a victory to ingenuity.
An escape.
The ball transforming the afternoon
into a fleeting sense of freedom.

Sara

Inspired by Sara Leicht-Weinstein

Sara remembers
black soot covering her face and body.
The smell of burning flesh.
Fire and smoke.
Indescribable stench.
The smoking chimneys.
The sound of the trains
and the children weeping.
Sara remembers her home.
Life before deportation and humiliation.
A simple life woven with
family and faith.
Sabbath dinners.
Weddings.
Births.
Circumcisions
and holidays.
Sara remembers her school shutting down.
All Jewish schools shutting down.
Returning home to see a yellow star in the window.
An alarming sight.
Sadness saturated the air,
on the last Seder before they left their house.
The keys were handed over at the town hall.
One suitcase for each of them.
Her father was a man of faith.
He dug a hole in the yard.
He buried a box with pictures,
candlesticks,
a menorah,

a kiddush cup,
documents,
and Sara's earrings.
A box for Sara to return to
her father said.
Decades passed.
Sara remembers
the trains.
The separation.
The ghetto.
The humiliation.
The murder of her family.
The slaughter of her people.
The enormous loss.
Her family's possessions plundered.
Sara gives her testimony willingly and generously.
She will continue as long as she lives and breathes.
She is not swallowed by the grief nor
the scars searing her soul.
She is a beacon of light.
Her resilience,
her courage,
Undeniable.

Two Hands

Two hands formed of stone
adorned the doors of the
old synagogue in Ukraine.
Once, scriptures were read.
Limbs swayed
in prayer.
Heads bowed.
Hymns were chanted and sung.
Laughter of children was heard.
Afterward, the perpetrators
piled their lifeless bodies without regard.
The walls that once saw joy
now witnessed sorrow.
A morgue.
A sea of bodies thrown, discarded.
The annihilation of a community
that once thrived.
Gone.

Ancestry

I chew small bites
of despair.
The mush
saturated with malice.
The alienation
of my ancestry.
A trail of crumbs.
A map of words interwoven with indescribable sorrow.
I stand outside of it.
Leaning.
For if I fall in, I may drown.
It's an ocean of muck.
An abyss.
It's stagnant,
rigid,
hard.
It's powerful.
It shrinks me with fear.
It threatens my existence.
"What if,"
surfaces on my lips.
What if?

The Righteousness Among Nations

The righteous
are a light in the dark.
Their humanity pumps blood into our hearts.
Ordinary people
doing extraordinary things,
inspired by an empathy rooted within.
Extending a hand to their fellow neighbors,
small and grand gestures.
An apple given,
a slice of bread,
a potato left behind.
Shelter during a roundup.
Harboring folk and risking a penalty
of imprisonment
or death.
The stories are endless, of rescues,
of displays of courage and humanity.
While the world looked away,
they rose to the challenge.

Transnistria

Human skeletons stagger
over the dead bodies.
Emaciated and frail,
their rage silenced.
Misery floats through them
like an illness gnawing in the bones.
Ghosts hover over the Dniester River.
Ghosts of men, women, and children.
Rounded up.
Accused of economic crimes.
Deported.
Murdered.
Ghosts hovering over Transnistria.
The name does not roll off the tongue easily.
Hell on earth ensued there.
Blood spilled in the streets.
Surviving was not living,
but existing.
The days were long,
The hours were endless.
The hunger was intolerable.
Transnistria.
The crimes committed there,
never to be forgotten.

Mourn

I mourn your childhood.
The one that was taken.
The one that
morphed into
an unrecognizable existence.
I mourn the fabric of your universe torn.
I mourn the hunger that became your companion.
I mourn the dark shadows of war upon you.
Huddled like matchsticks in cattle cars.
I mourn the fear that took you from home
into the forests walking for miles parched and ravenous.
I mourn the slaughter of your kin,
the sorrow and heartbreak.
I mourn your world crumbling into small fragments.
The smell of decay spreading.
The familiar vanished.
The insecurity flourished.
The lack of safety as
your interior world disintegrated
and life was decomposed.

Acknowledgments

Gratitude to my publisher Golden Dragonfly Press.
Gratitude to my editor and friend Alice Maldonado.
Gratitude to my Online Community.
Gratitude to Daniel Zarfjian. The first reader of my poems. The editor and critic with a keen eye for the details.
Gratitude to my family. Those that came before and those after.
My parents for their unwavering love.
My grandparents Saba Naftali, Safta Dora. Saba Yancu, Safta Ginca.
Gratitude to my tribe of sisters. The strong women who always have my back.
A special thanks and love to Aunt Shelley that shared her impossible memories with me.

www.ingramcontent.com/pod-product-compliance
Lightning Source LLC
LaVergne TN
LVHW091317080426
835510LV00007B/531